THE GOSPEL DAY BY DAY
THROUGH ADVENT

The Gospel day by day through Advent

BRIAN MOORE SJ

A Liturgical Press Book

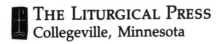

THE LITURGICAL PRESS
Collegeville, Minnesota

Cover by Fred Petters

Printed in the United States of America.

1	2	3	4	5	6	7	8	9

Library of Congress Cataloging-in-Publication Data

Moore, Brian A.
    The Gospel day by day through Advent / Brian Moore.
        p. cm.
    ISBN 0-8146-2001-9
    1. Advent—Prayer-books and devotions—English. 2. Bible. N.T.
Gospels—Liturgical lessons, English. I. Title.
BX2170.A4M667   1991
242'.33—dc20   91-22658
                                           CIP

Contents

Introduction   7

PHASE ONE   11

An Over-view   13

First Week of Advent   17
Sunday, Year A   17
Sunday, Year B   18
Sunday, Year C   20
Monday   21
Tuesday   23
Wednesday   24
Thursday   26
Friday   27
Saturday   29

PHASE TWO   31

An Over-view   33

Second Week of Advent   37
Sunday, Year A   37
Sunday, Year B   38
Sunday, Year C   40
Monday   41
Tuesday   43
Wednesday   44
Thursday   46
Friday   47
Saturday   49

Third Week of Advent   51
Sunday, Year A   51
Sunday, Year B   52
Sunday, Year C   54
Monday   55
Tuesday   57
Wednesday   58
Thursday   60
Friday   61

PHASE THREE   63

An Over-view   65

Fourth Week of Advent   67
Sunday, Year A   67
Sunday, Year B   68
Sunday, Year C   70

December 17th   71
December 18th   73
December 19th   73
December 20th   74
December 21st   75
December 22nd   75
December 23rd   76
December 24th   78

Introduction

Of all the Seasons of the Church's Liturgical Year, Advent (it seems to me) is the one with which it is most difficult to live in harmony of spirit. For one thing, the world of commerce intrudes both early and noisily. The Season has hardly begun (if, indeed, it has so much as begun) when on all sides we are bombarded with the sights and sounds of Christmas — urgent reminders, with a day-by-day countdown, of how close the Festival is, constant solicitings to purchase our readiness for it. It is easy enough, perhaps, to close our eyes and ears to such sights and sounds; it is not so easy to insulate our minds from a preoccupation with the gifts and greetings which Christmas requires of us. A final difficulty which the Season of Advent presents is that its first phase is a consideration of the Second Coming of Christ in power and majesty and judgement. The first phase of Advent, therefore, may seem to be little more than a prolongation of the theme of the closing weeks of the just concluded Ordinary Time.

To recognise that these difficulties exist is a first, and considerable, step in off-setting them, so that we can, in our prayer, maintain (as Vatican II requires) Advent's specific character, so that it and the other Liturgical Seasons, 'duly nourish the piety of the faithful who celebrate the mysteries of Christian redemption'. An over-view of the structure of the whole Season of Advent is a simple, and perhaps the best, way of revealing that Season's 'specific character'. The first thing which appears from such an over-view is that Advent is not simply a time of preparation for Christmas. The Season, in fact, puts before us for our meditation three distinct, but necessarily inter-connected, 'comings' of Christ. The structure, and thereby the inner dynamic, of the Season may be laid out as follows:

SUNDAY	YEAR	READING	THEME
		PHASE ONE	
1	A	Mt 24:37-44	Watchfulness for
	B	Mt 13:33-37	Christ's coming
	C	Lk 21:25-28, 34-36	in Judgement
		PHASE TWO	
2	A	Mt 3:1-12	John the Baptist proclaims
	B	Mk 1:1-8	the imminent appearance
	C	Lk 3:1-6	of the Christ
3	A	Mt 11:2-11	John the Baptist bears
	B	Jn 1:6-8, 19-28	witness that Jesus is
	C	Lk 3:10-18	the Christ
		PHASE THREE	
4	A	Mt 1:18-25	The Word-made-flesh is about
	B	Lk 1:26-38	to come into the world, being
	C	Lk 1:39-45	born, in time, of the Virgin Mary

The Season culminates on Christmas Day, and during the eight days which precede the Feast the Gospel Readings recall the events leading up to the Nativity at Bethlehem: (*)

(*) Note: These eight days are called 'Late Advent Weekdays', and the Readings appointed for them take the place of those of the weekdays on which those dates fall. *Sundays are unaffected*. These dates can begin as early as the Third Sunday of Advent and as late as the Saturday after the Third Sunday. This book gives reflections for the weekdays up to that Saturday, as well as for each of the Late Advent Weekdays. The user of this book needs to keep an eye on a liturgical calendar of the current year.

DATE	READING	THEME
17	Mt 1:1-17	The human ancestry of Christ
18	Mt 1:18-24	The virginal conception of Christ and the annunciation of this to St Joseph
19	Lk 1:5-25	The annunciation of the conception of John the Baptist
20	Lk 1:26-38	The annunciation to Mary
21	Lk 1:39-45	Mary's visitation of Elizabeth
22	Lk 1:46-56	Mary's canticle, the *Magnificat*
23	Lk 1:57-66	The birth and naming of John the Baptist
24	Lk 1:67-79	Canticle of Zechariah, the *Benedictus*

In keeping with the above Tables, what follows is divided into three *Phases*, each of which is further divided into (a) a general over-view of the *Phase*, (b) a reflection on the Gospel Readings of each Sunday within the *Phase*, and (c) a reflection on the Gospel Reading of each weekday within the *Phase*.

PHASE ONE
First Week of Advent

An Over-view
The Return of Christ in Judgement

The Gospel passages appointed for reading on the First Sunday of Advent are quite brief. Their theme is *watchfulness* — in view of the uncertainty of the hour of the Lord's coming. The Reading for Year A concludes with, 'Therefore, be you also in readiness, for the Son of Man is to come at an hour unknown to you'. In the Reading for Year B, in a few verses, Jesus three times urges his hearers, 'Stay awake'. In Year C, the warning is given, 'Stay awake . . . praying at all times'.

This teaching of Jesus in the Gospels is faithfully reflected by the Apostles in their Epistles. Peter (in 2 Pet 3:10) and Paul (in Thess 5:2) assert that the Day of the Lord will come like a thief in the night — using the image Jesus himself first proposed in his parable about the wakeful householder (in Lk 12:39).

The Scriptures' teaching on the Coming of the Lord refers, in the first place, to the return of Christ in glory and in judgement. This exhortation to watchfulness, then, is addressed, in the first place, to the whole pilgrim Church. Equally, however, it is addressed to every follower of Christ. The aim of the exhortation is not to inspire fear of the unknown; its object is to keep us from growing slack in the service of Christ. In Mt 24:48-51, Jesus warns up not to be like the servant who says in his heart, 'My master is delaying his coming', and falls to lording it over his fellow servants and to regaling his boon companions with his master's goods. On the contrary, Jesus urges us (in Lk 12:35-37) to 'be dressed for service and have lighted lamps in your hands, to be like servants awaiting their master's return'.

This kind of 'watchfulness' consists in leading a good life as servants of Christ. So Peter (in 2 Pet 3:11-12) reminds us that since everything will have an end we must live a good and holy life as we wait and long for the Lord's coming, adding, 'Therefore, dear friends, strive to be spotless and upright, so that he will find you at peace'. Paul (in 1 Thess 3:12-13) prays for us that the Lord would confirm our hearts in holiness so that we may be found blameless in his sight when he comes again. John (in 1 Jn 2:28) begs us to 'remain in him, so that when he comes we may have confidence and not turn from him in shame at his coming'.

If, in the context of the Second Coming, 'watchfulness' has its own special urgency and its own special nature, it has, also, its particular spirit. From the above quotations from the Apostles (as also we find in James 5:7-8) it is evident that the people to whom these words were addressed were presumed to be filled with longing for, even impatient for, the coming of the Day of the Lord.

This is the spirit which the Liturgy would have us cultivate. The first of the Prefaces for Advent declares that we watch for the Day because we hold to the hope of salvation when Christ returns in glory; and, at every Mass, in the prayer following the Lord's Prayer, we pray to be kept free from sin (which is the essence of 'watching') and free from all anxiety as we *do* wait — for the coming of our Saviour is not a fear but a joyful hope we entertain. This spirit we learn from Jesus himself who (in Lk 21:28-31) speaks of the signs of his coming and tells us that then we should 'look aloft and lift up our heads, for our redemption is at hand'.

The image which Jesus here puts before us — that of a tree putting forth first its green leaves and then its fruit — is very appropriate, significant as it is of life and fruitfulness; for in comparison with the transformation which will be wrought in us at Christ's coming and the glory that will then be ours (cf. 2 Cor 3:18 and Phil 3:21) we are at present but barren stock.

In the Eucharist there is made present to us He who was and is to come (cf Rev 1:4) for every time the Eucharist is celebrated we show forth the death of the Lord until he comes again (cf. 1 Cor 11:26). In the early Church, therefore, the expectation was that the Second Coming would occur during the celebration of the Eucharist, and considerable use was made of the acclamation, 'Marana tha', meaning, 'Come, our Lord!' (This acclamation is to be found, also, in the conclusion to the First Letter to the Corinthians and to the Book of Revelation.)

This first phase of Advent, then, invites us to deepen our appreciation of the Eucharist as a celebration of a reality which is yet to be, as well as the memorial of the Lord's death in the past and a celebration of his real presence to us in the sacred Mysteries. It is a time, too, in which to examine ourselves to see if our hearts truly entertain, and our lives proclaim, that 'joyful hope' which should be the hallmark of a follower of Christ — a time to see if we truly reject that most un-Christian thing, anxiety, through genuine and complete trust in the Lord.

Finally, Advent is a time in which to detach our hearts more resolutely from anything they cling to which would make us less than prepared for, less than desirous of his Coming.

First Sunday of Advent
Year A
Matthew 24:37-44

The whole of the chapter from which today's Gospel Reading is taken consists of Jesus' discourse on 'the last times'.

It begins with a rather terrible note of finality: 'Jesus left the Temple' — that Temple doomed to destruction within a few decades. Jesus' leaving the Temple signifies the end of the Old Covenant; and the subsequent destruction of the Temple serves as a symbol of the 'end time'. For then, the return of Christ will manifest God's judgement upon the whole human race, just as the destruction of Jerusalem is seen as God's judgement on the chosen race.

On that day, Jesus says, the Son of Man will send his angels to gather his chosen from every quarter of the earth. This verse (v. 31) indicates the meaning of what we read in today's passage: 'one is taken' — that is, taken up into definitive salvation; 'one is left' — left, that is, to judgement and condemnation.

What differentiates the 'taken' from the 'left' has nothing to do with any earthly status: both men are equally engaged in earning their livelihood; both women are equally engaged in their domestic tasks. Yet one is 'taken', the other 'left'. This is because it is a question here of God's judgement, not of human perceptions.

Jesus recalls the days of Noah and the Flood. The people of that time, in the vignette Jesus here gives of them, were doing nothing one could think of as evil (eating, drinking, marrying) just as the men in the field and the women at the mill will be doing ordinary, everyday things.

What distinguished Noah from his contemporaries was his readiness for God's visitation. What distinguishes the 'taken' from the 'left' is, likewise, readiness. The thing which militates against this readiness is not our human activity, our particular way of life; it is indifference to 'the Day of his coming' — an indifference which arises from absorption in even the most innocent of pleasures and fruitful labours of the daily round.

Life can be lived only from day to day (whether the prospect of yet another day be pleasurable or painful) yet each day has to be lived within the context of *the* Day. This awareness is not meant to create an atmosphere of anxiety; rather, it gives point and purpose to our everyday living.

Just so, the return of 'the Son of Man on the clouds of heaven with power and great glory' (v. 30) finally reveals the point and purpose of the birth of a Child in a stable at Bethlehem.

First Sunday of Advent
Year B
Mark 13:33-37

The conclusion of today's Reading, 'What I say to you I say to all', may leave us wondering who comprised the 'you' — while we know full well that we are included in the 'all'. We find the answer in the third verse of the complete chapter from which this Reading is taken.

The 'you' are the two pairs of brothers among the Apostles: Peter and Andrew, James and John. They are alone with Jesus, who is 'sitting opposite the Temple' which he has just left. What are the thoughts of his heart at this moment, one wonders, since he has just now foretold the destruction of that Temple — his Father's house, in which he had been presented as a new-born baby, was found as a child, had taught as a man, which he had cleansed in anger and which, finally, he had 'left' (cf. 1st Sunday: Year A).

With the mysterious omission of Andrew, these are the same Apostles who witness the Transfiguration of Jesus, and his Agony in the Garden. Of that first occasion, Luke says: 'Peter and his companions were heavy with sleep, but they kept awake and saw his glory . . . ' Of the second occasion, all three Evangelists who record the incident testify that these Apostles slept — even though Jesus had urged them, 'Keep awake'. There is, therefore, a special poignancy in Jesus' exhortation in today's Reading. In the space of only five verses he three times says, 'Stay awake', in addition to the urging, 'Be on your guard'.

In this handful of verses, Mark gathers together very powerfully the essence of a number of Jesus' parables. Recalling them makes us realise how constant throughout his preaching is his impressing upon us the need for watchfulness — not only with a view to his Second Coming but also with a view to our being alert to, and heedful of, his coming to us in our day to day lives as, through his Spirit, he prompts us to do good and avoid evil.

Thus, Jesus' words, 'Be on your guard' recall his parable of the householder and the burglar (Mt 24:23). His reference to the man travelling abroad reminds us of a similar parable in Mt 24:45-51. And the master of the house who may return during any one of the four 'watches' of the night (evening, midnight, cockcrow, dawn) recalls both the master returning from the wedding feast (Lk 12:35-38) and the parable of the Ten Bridesmaids (the Wise and Foolish Virgins) in Mt 25:1-13.

The object of all these exhortations to vigilance is not to cause us to live in an atmosphere of fear or of timidity of spirit. It is to our own advantage that we be attentive to the various ways in which Jesus comes into our lives — most commonly in the form of people in need. Jesus himself wept over Jerusalem because it did not recognise the day of its being visited.

Recounting the incident of the Transfiguration, Luke noted that the Apostles were heavy with sleep but stayed awake and saw Jesus' glory. We, too, combat the heaviness of disinterest or timidity for the ultimate purpose of, ourselves also, seeing his glory.

19

First Sunday of Advent
Year C
Luke 21:25-28, 34-36

Here Jesus speaks (as we ourselves do) in imagery derived from one of the strands of the religious tradition in which both he and his hearers were raised. The portents in the sky and on the earth and human reaction to them (and, thereby, to what unknown terrors they might portend) are, in the Old Testament, common symbols of divine intervention in the course of human history.

It is natural, therefore, that Jesus uses such language when he affirms that he will come again, and that in his coming will bring the whole order of created things and human history to their predestined consummation.

The images he uses are called 'signs'; but they are not signs in the sense of such folk wisdom as, 'Red morning, shepherd's warning'. Consequently, looking for verification of them in the events of anyone's lifetime is pointless — as Jesus himself says earlier in this chapter (cf. vs. 8-9). They are simply images of the cosmic dimensions of definitive divine intervention in creation and human affairs.

A pinpointing of the Old Testament origin of these images is interesting, but of no great importance. What matters is a conviction of the truth they intend to convey — in the angels' words at the Ascension, '. . . this same Jesus will return . . .'.

Important, too, is our personal reaction to that conviction. We are not to be people 'dying of fear as they await what menaces the world'. On the contrary, our faith in the return of Jesus should cause us to 'stand erect, heads held high' — as people stand when they are confident, joyful, full of expectation.

The reason for this is that, for those who believe in him, Jesus' return is not a 'menace', a threat to inspire 'fear unto death'.

On the contrary, it is the prelude to the believers' 'liberation', their deliverance, their redemption.

In our daily eucharistic Liturgy we offer a prayer which expresses precisely the spirit of today's Reading:

> Deliver us, Lord, from every evil (cf. v. 36) . . . keep us free from sin (cf. v. 34) and protect us from all anxiety as we wait in joyful hope for the coming of our Saviour, Jesus Christ (cf. v. 28).

The logical connection between this 'joyful hope' and the injunction to live a moral life which, in this Reading, immediately follows is well expressed by John (in 1 Jn 3:3):

> Surely everyone who entertains this hope must purify himself, must try to be as pure as Christ.

Hence, Jesus here warns us against 'coarseness of heart' — that insensitivity to spiritual realities which, in the words of Peter (2 Pet 3:3) leads to making fun of the promise, as it does to indifference towards its fulfilment. Against such hardening of the heart, the only remedies are vigilance over oneself, and prayer — as today's Reading, in concluding, points out.

First Week
Monday
Matthew 8:5-13

Sometimes Jesus works a miracle simply out of the impulse of his compassionate heart — appealed to or, even, unasked. But generally his miracles are worked for a further purpose: for example, as a sign (and this is so especially in John's gospel) — as when he raises someone from the dead in token of his power to raise from spiritual death.

Here, as most commonly, the working of the miracle is inseparably linked with faith in Jesus — either in the petitioner or in the recipient; and this necessity of having faith points beyond the miracle itself to the necessity of having faith in Jesus

21

in order to receive the greater gratuity of admission into the Kingdom, where all ills are healed.

It is in the last few verses of today's Reading, therefore, not so much in the miracle itself, that we see the suitability of it as an apt illustration of the spirit of this first phase of Advent.

The centurion (Christ-like in his compassion for his ailing servant) is also a striking illustration of sheer faith in Jesus. His being a centurion means that he is a Roman soldier; but his being an officer in the army of occupation of a conquered country does not prejudice him against a member of the conquered people. This is in sharp contrast with that people's leaders whose prejudice against a section of their own race is a chief obstacle to their accepting Jesus. Quite bluntly (in Jn 7:52, for example) they assert, 'Prophets do not come out of Galilee', as Jesus did.

The centurion knows all about authority — and he has seen it in Jesus. He knows all about the exercise of authority — it is the word of command not the presence of the commander that produces the effect. Hence his magnificent profession of faith: '... say but the word ...'.

Jesus marvels at the depth of the centurion's faith — a simple and complete trust in Jesus and the power of his word — and contrasts it with what he finds in the leaders of his own nation, who are forever demanding signs and questioning his authority. Consequently, he takes his opportunity to state quite clearly the necessity of faith, insisting that mere physical descent from Abraham, the simple fact of belonging to the chosen race ('the subjects of the kingdom' of verse 12) is no longer relevant. Exclusion from his Kingdom does not come from being born a gentile. This is the assertion (grateful to our ears, shocking to his hearers) of verse 11. Exclusion comes from rejecting him, for to do so implies the wish to have no seat at the feast which is his Kingdom (v. 11).

Only those who humble themselves in the self-abandonment of faith in Jesus will be exalted.

First Week
Tuesday
Luke 10:21-24

At this point in his public life, Jesus is welcoming back the seventy-two disciples he had sent out in pairs 'to all the towns and places he himself was to visit'. Thus the vocation of John the Baptist — 'to prepare the way of the Lord' — is extended, just as, through those who believe in him (and this includes us ourselves) Jesus' own task of proclaiming the Good News is to be carried on 'into the whole world' and 'until the end of time' — that time to which, in this phase of Advent, we look forward in 'joyful hope'.

Joy abounds in this chapter of Luke's gospel. 'The seventy-two came back rejoicing': they had found that, in Jesus' name, they had power over even the devils. Jesus encourages them to rejoice, rather, that their names are written in heaven.

And Jesus himself rejoices in the Spirit, is 'filled with joy by the Holy Spirit'. It reminds us of Mary at the Visitation, of Elizabeth on the same occasion, of Simeon at the Presentation in the Temple. For joy of this kind is one of the fruits of the Holy Spirit (cf. Gal 5:22). Such a joy is not a vapid cheerfulness; it is a deep, serene happiness which springs from the hope that, through our faith in Jesus, our names, too, are 'written in heaven', and that at his Second Coming we ourselves shall 'be taken up to meet the Lord and stay with him for ever' (cf. 1 Thess 4:17).

As with the principals at the Visitation and Presentation, so with Jesus here: a sign that our joy is of the Holy Spirit is that its issues in praise of God — whom Jesus here addresses as 'Father'. And very soon (in 11:1-4) he will teach his followers to use the same manner of address in their own prayers.

23

By his words here regarding the uniqueness of the mutual knowledge of the Father and the Son, Jesus reveals the uniqueness of his relationship of sonship with the Father. By his teaching his followers to join him in addressing God as 'Father', Jesus reveals the relationship which exists between himself and his followers. They who believe in him are thereby identified with him.

Jesus turns to his disciples, saying, 'Happy the eyes which see what you see'. He probably means the fulfilment of the prophecies and the coming of salvation. However, what the disciples are seeing at that very moment is the face of Jesus — 'the Word made flesh, full of grace and truth'.

In this life, we, by faith, look upon the face of Jesus — in the joyful hope that at his coming , all veils removed, we shall behold him face to face in all his glory.

First Week
Wednesday
Matthew 15:29-37

In the incidents narrated in today's Reading, Jesus heals and feeds. The Reading is, therefore, very appropriate to this first phase of Advent; for, in his Second Coming, Jesus will heal all ills, and will invite into the feast of everlasting life all who are willing to take their place in it.

The Reading suggests, therefore, that an essential part of our personal living-out the spirit of Advent is that we discern what are our hurts (those things of which we feel the need of healing) and what are our hungers (those longings of which we desire the satisfying): and not only our own, but those of others — in order to be more like him whom we profess to follow, and who says of himself, 'I have compassion . . . '.

We visualise the scene of healing. Jesus has gone 'up the hillside', and the sick are laid 'at his feet'. Surely Matthew means us to recall Isaiah (in 52:7), 'How beautiful upon the mountains are the feet of one who brings good news, who heralds peace, brings happiness, proclaims salvation'. Just such healing — the blind seeing, the dumb speaking, the lame walking — was the answer Jesus gave to the enquirers whom John the Baptist, then imprisoned, had sent to him with the question, 'Are you the One?' (cf. Lk 7:22).

This recalling of Isaiah also recalls that prophet's insistance that salvation is not the exclusive prerogative of Israel but is to be extended to the Gentiles also. And here, both in the geographical setting of the incident and in the fact that the crowd, astonished at the cures, 'praised the God *of Israel*', there is the suggestion that this crowd as a whole is composed not of Jews but of Gentiles — drawn to Jesus, perhaps, by rumours of the miracle which he had wrought for the woman of Canaan which Matthew relates immediately before today's Reading (in vs. 21-28).

Healing, then; and, then, the feasting. Those few loaves — the final outcome of sowing, reaping, grinding, kneading, baking — are truly 'the work of human hands'. But, surrendered into the hands of Jesus they feed thousands. Of these loaves, Matthew writes that Jesus took them, gave thanks, broke them, and gave them to his disciples.

His action here precisely forecasts both the institution of the Eucharist at the Last Supper, and its continuation in the Liturgy of his Church — in which it becomes *the* symbol of the feast of everlasting life in the Kingdom, to the coming of which we, in Advent, look forward.

But the distribution of the broken bread is left to the disciples. That is to say, Jesus has committed, together with himself, his earthly mission into the hands and mouths of his followers.

First Week
Thursday
Matthew 7:24-27

The few verses which comprise today's Reading are the final words of that teaching of Jesus which we call The Sermon on the Mount. This teaching begins with Mt 5:1: 'Seeing the crowds, he went up the hill . . . Then he began to speak.' The verse immediately following today's Reading is Matthew's comment, 'Jesus had now finished what he wanted to say, and his teaching made a deep impression on the people because he taught with authority' — that is to say, his *own* authority — 'and not like their own scribes' — who simply quoted and commented on traditional 'authorities'.

What today's Reading alerts us to, however, is that receiving 'a deep impression' is not enough.

When the five foolish bridesmaids, knocking at the closed door of the banqueting hall, cried our, 'Lord, Lord open the door for us', the Lord replied, 'I do not know you' (Mt 25:1-13). Others will remind him, 'We once ate and drank in your company; you taught in our streets'; and the Lord will reply, 'I do not know you' (Lk 13:25-27). Still others will protest, 'Lord, Lord, did we not prophesy, cast out demons, work many miracles — all in your name?' They, too, are answered with 'I have never known you' (Mt 7:22-23); that is to say, You were never mine.

'When that day comes' (v. 22), the day of Judgement at the Second Coming, mere lip service will be exposed for the falsity it always was. The only thing that will count is whether or not we have based our lives on a genuine acceptance of Jesus' teaching, and have acted accordingly — being among those who listen to his words and act upon them (v. 24). Not to have done so will be to have entered by the wrong gate, to have chosen the wrong road (vs. 13-14).

By omitting verses 22 and 23, today's Reading brings resolutely together (and makes identical) 'the person who does the will of my Father in heaven' and 'the one who listens to these words of mine and acts on them'. That is to say, when Jesus teaches us what we should be and do, he is teaching us what is the will of God for us.

So the Father himself had proclaimed at Jesus' baptism by John: 'This is my Son; listen to him'. So Jesus, when (in Jn 6:28-30) he is asked, 'What must we do if we are to do the works that God wants of us?', answers, 'Believe in the One he has sent'. And his hearers, by promptly demanding a sign, acknowledge that he is speaking about himself.

There are only two gates, two roads, two foundations on which to build — acceptance of or rejection of Jesus and the values he teaches. The choice of one will not prevent us muddling our way through this life; but only the right choice will enable us to stand in the Day of his Coming.

First Week
Friday
Matthew 9:27-31

That 'then the eyes of the blind shall be opened' is one of the images used by Isaiah to signify that 'Your God is coming . . . he is coming to save you' (Is 35:4-5). To this Old Testament passage Jesus himself draws his hearers' attention when he assures the messengers whom John the Baptist had sent to him that he was, indeed, the One-who-was-to-come (cf. Mt 11:4).

In his teaching, Jesus frequently uses blindness as a symbol of unbelief: people can be physically sighted, but spiritually blind — or the reverse, as in today's Reading, where the blind men affirm both that Jesus is the Son of David (the Messiah) and that he has the power to heal them. It is only when spiritual blindness is deliberate, its presence denied, that healing is impossible. When people trust (blindly) in their own light, their own wisdom, refusing belief in the Light and Word whom the Father has sent into the world, then their end can only be in darkness and confusion.

When, therefore, Jesus says to his disciples, 'Blessed are your eyes for they see' (cf. 1st Week: Tuesday) he is commending not their physical association with him in his ministry but their spiritual insight — their faith in him.

Those two great, brief prayers, 'Lord, that I may see!' (Lk 18:41) and, 'Lord, help my unbelief!' (Mk 9:24) are, on one level, identical.

These two prayers should be constantly ours also so that we become of the company of Zaccheus, climbing his tree in order that 'he might see Jesus who he was', and of the Greeks who, on the eve of the Lord's passion, come to Philip saying, 'Sir, we would see Jesus' — not with the eyes of the body but of the soul, not with the light of sight but of faith. For during his life on earth many saw Jesus, but few saw 'who he was' — since only faith can reveal that. To have lived, literally, in the time of our Lord as a contemporary is not necessarily an advantage. It is enough to be living in Faith in the time of the Lord who is with us always, according to his promise.

Jesus, 'God from God, Light from Light', is the 'true light who enlightens everyone who comes into this world' (Jn 1:9). Consequently he says of himself, 'As long as I am in the world I am the light of the world' (Jn 9:5), and he begs us, 'While you have the light believe in the light that you may be sons of the light' (Jn 12:36). Faith is crucial, for 'we walk by faith and not by sight' (2 Cor 5:7); and the judgement passed on this world is that people preferred darkness to the light (Jn 3:17-21). That is to say, they refused belief; and their refusal of belief stemmed from the fact that 'their deeds were evil', and they were unwilling to make that radical change in the values they held and their ways of acting which belief in Jesus requires.

First Week
Saturday
Matthew 9:35, 10:1,6-8

Essentially, what today's Reading does is to assure us that Jesus' own ministry of proclaiming the Good News and of healing will continue in our world until he comes again. It is, therefore, a fitting reading to bring this first phase of Advent to its conclusion.

Jesus gives his disciples a share in his own authority and a share in his own mission. For the time being, he also places on them the same restriction his Father had placed on him. Here he says, 'Go only to the lost sheep of the House of Israel', as elsewhere he says of himself (in Mt 15:24), 'I was sent only to the lost sheep of the House of Israel'. All these details serve to emphasise the continuity between Jesus' ministry and that of his Church.

Clearly, Jesus would also have those who carry on his ministry to do so in the same spirit as he himself did — a spirit of compassion for a world of people lost and lacking direction, 'harassed and dejected like sheep without a shepherd', and such a spirit of self-sacrifice as leads a disciple of his to look for no personal reward but freely to give of what has been freely received.

Expressly limited in scope for a time, the Twelve, and the Church whose foundation stones they are, will just as expressly be given a universal mission in the command, 'Go, therefore; make disciples of all the nations ... And know that I am with you always' (Mt 28:19-20). This presence of Jesus to the labourers in his harvest is not simply a presence in their hearts through their faith in their Lord; it is an active, co-operative presence: 'Going out they preached everywhere, the Lord working with them . . .' (Mk 16:20).

Throughout the time which will elapse until he comes again, Jesus seeks people to work with him in the proclamation of the Good News and in healing human hurting. In the face of the immensity of this task — the greatness of the harvest — he bids us pray the Lord of the harvest to send labourers to gather in the increase.

This prayer is more than 'prayer for vocations' as we commonly say, understanding thereby the sacred ministry and the religious life. It is, in fact, prayer that all Jesus' followers (and we are numbered among them) will realise their various vocations.

Not only is there, among the People of God, a universal call to personal holiness, there is also a universal call to take one's part in the 'missionary' activity of the Church; so that all, in their personal lives, bear witness to Jesus, and prove to be good advertisements (so to speak) for the Good News and for the peace and healing reconciliation which embracing and living-out that Good News can bring.

PHASE TWO
Second and Third Weeks of Advent

An Over-view
The Christ and his Precursor

The Gospel Readings for the second and third Sundays of Advent are devoted to the part played by John the Baptist in the beginning of Jesus' public ministry — the second of the three comings of Jesus into the world of human affairs which Advent commemorates. The Baptist's two-fold role is summed up in the second Preface of Advent: 'John the Baptist was his Herald' (and this is the theme of the Gospel Reading for the Second Sunday) 'and made him known when at last he came' (the theme of the Gospel of the Third Sunday).

Recalling the Baptist's preaching reminds us how we are so to accept Christ and his teaching in our daily lives that 'when he comes we may have confidence, and not turn from him in shame at his coming' (1 Jn 2:28).

While Jesus grew to mature manhood in the normal circumstances of an artisan's house in an obscure provincial town, John 'lived out in the wilderness until the day he appeared openly to Israel' (Lk 1:80). But then, 'In the wilderness, the word of God came to John' (Lk 3:2) — and he knew that he was to be the voice which long ago Isaiah had foretold: 'A voice crying in the wilderness, "Prepare a way for the Lord; make straight his paths"' (Lk 3:4). Obedient to God's call, John began preaching throughout the whole Jordan district, and there gathered around him a close band of disciples. To these he taught his own asceticism of prayer and fasting (Lk 5:33). His exhortations to the people at large had the same end in view — 'repentence'. By this he meant a radical change of heart — the acceptance of which was symbolised by acceptance of the baptism he performed but was expressed not by a radical change of life-style but by a blamelessness of conduct within any chosen (or enforced) way of life.

He taught his hearers charity to the poor: 'You have two tunics? Give one to someone who has none. You have food? Give to someone who has none' (Lk 3:11). To him came the despised tax-collectors: 'Master,' they said, 'what must we do?' John replied, 'Demand no more than the prescribed taxes' (Lk 3:12). When soldiers asked him the same question, John answered: 'No violence. No trumped-up charges. Be satisfied with your pay' (Lk 3:14).

It is hard to imagine the impact of John's teaching on souls who sought God but who found in their religious leaders, for the most part, only legalism, rigorism and formalism. Later, Jesus himself would indict them:

Woe to you, scribes and Pharisees, hypocrites! For you close the Kingdom of Heaven against men. For you neither go in yourselves nor permit those who would go in to enter' (Mt 23:13).

John's teaching brought his hearers hope: the Kingdom of Heaven is closed to no one, no matter what his calling, if only he will repent of his sins, practice charity, and sin no more. It is hardly to be wondered at that vast crowds heard him willingly and conjectured that he might, in fact, be the long-promised, long-desired Messiah.

What the Liturgy of the Second Sunday of Advent does, in effect, is to assure us that, as Vatican II says, the call to holiness is addressed to all — including ourselves. We are not (whether out of timidity or sloth) to entertain the thought either that we as individuals are not called to seek holiness of life or that our particular calling in life puts insurmountable obstacles in the way of our achieving it. But, as John warned his hearers, this implies a readiness to accept into lives the Christ who was coming and the baptism in the Spirit which he would confer.

In the course of his preaching he said, 'Someone is coming after me who is more powerful than I am, and I am not fit to kneel down and undo the strap of his sandals. I have baptised you with water, but he will baptise you with the Holy Spirit' (Mk 1:7-8).

———————

The Gospel Reading for the Third Sunday of Advent tells us that John bore witness that Jesus was, indeed, the Son of God, the Christ, the Chosen, the Beloved. The passage from John's Gospel (Jn 1:6-8, 19-28) does this by quoting the Baptist's reply to the priests and Levites who questioned him as to who he was; the passage from Matthew (Mt 11:2-11) does it by quoting Jesus' assertion that John had fulfilled his mission as Herald; and the passage from Luke does it by quoting the Baptist's response to the crowd's surmise that John himself might be the Christ (Lk 3:10-18).

The extracts from the Gospels set down for the weekdays following this Sunday contain a number of eulogies of John pronounced by Jesus at various times in his 'public life'. These commend John as having been 'a true pattern of righteousness' (Mt 21:32) and 'a lamp alight and shining' who 'gave his testimony to the truth' (cf. Jn 5:33-36).

What Jesus commends in John he also looks to find in his followers — personal holiness, and fidelity to whatever it is that God calls us to in our own lives.

In this respect, our whole life needs to be lived in the Advent spirit of watchfulness — of readiness to perceive what is the will of God for us and a readiness to do it. In this, John the Baptist is a model for us.

For over thirty years he pursued righteousness; and when 'the word of the Lord came to him in the wilderness' he obeyed it promptly and gave himself to the one, short-lived task God appointed him.

Luke, in quoting Jesus' exhortation, 'Be watchful', adds the words, 'praying at all times'. Prayer is essential not only to growing in the Spirit, to making progress in the spiritual life, but also for discerning what is the will of God for us. If our hearts are not watchful in prayer we will miss the day of his coming to us as (through the circumstances of our daily life or through other people or through the promptings of his Spirit) he lets us know what he would have of us.

This second phase of Advent, then, is more than simply a recalling of the preaching of John the Baptist and his witness to Christ. It also reminds us of the call we receive to pursue holiness and to discern the will of God for us. In doing so, we prepare for the Second Coming of the Lord; but to do so requires that 'watchfulness' which is the dominant theme of the first phase of this sacred Season.

Second Sunday of Advent
Year A
Matthew 3:1-12

'In those days, John the Baptist appeared, preaching ... '
It sounds quite casual, as if these things, quite arbitrarily, simply happened. But it was not so. John's appearing was not a result of some impule of self-will; nor was the content of his preaching a wisdom of his own.

Far from it. 'A man came, *sent* by God. His name was John' (Jn 1:6). John the Baptist appeared when he did because God called him at that particular time. That time is pin-pointed by Luke in a kind of 'Who was Who' in those days: Tiberius in Rome, Pilate in Judea, Herod in Galilee, Philip in Ituraea, Lysanias in Abilene, Annas and Caiphas in Jerusalem (cf. Lk 3:1-2). They comprise the whole contemporary array of political and priestly power of whom Jesus (whose imminent coming John is to proclaim) will fall foul. Christianity is rooted in human history, and history repeats itself.

At that precise time, 'the word of God came to John ... in the wilderness' — that word being both the call to 'go public', and the assurance that his long years of solitary meditation on the Prophets were over, and that the time of their fulfilment was *now*. John knew then that he was to be (in quite another sense than in the original) Isaiah's 'voice crying in the wilderness, ''Prepare the way of the Lord'' '.

John's was the attentive ear of the true disciple, and his, consequently, was 'a disciple's tongue' (cf. Is 50:4-5).

It is by attentive listening in the silence of prayer that we, too, in our time, will come to understand the will of God for us and the time of our fulfilling it.

John then appears — dressed in the fashion of Elijah who, it was popularly believed, was to return to herald the coming of the Messiah. In preparation for that coming, John preaches 'repentance'. 'Repentance' means a complete change of heart — a change which demands an openness to accept, simply on his own word, what the Messiah will say. All former preconceptions of what salvation means must be jettisoned in favour of pure faith in Jesus, together with all hither-to embraced assurances — even descent from Abraham.

This radical change of heart is, of course, wholly within; but *that* it has taken place can be manifested exteriorally — first in acceptance of John's baptism, and then in bringing forth 'the appropriate fruit'.

Our own baptism is something which can not be repeated; yet, each year at Easter, the Church asks us to renew our commitment to that giving of ourselves wholly to Christ which baptism implies. That 'repentence', that change of heart called for by both John and Jesus himself, is a continuing thing, something to be deepened daily.

This deepening of the Christ-centredness of our lives is the principal preoccupation of Advent — whether in preparation for the Second Coming of Jesus, or his first.

Second Sunday of Advent
Year B
Mark 1:1-8

Mark is a man of few words, and he is not given to using them pointlessly.

In verse 1 he abruptly announces, 'The beginning of the Good News about Jesus Christ'. From the outset, therefore, he signals that the verses which follow are not so much about John the Baptist, whom they introduce, as about Jesus, whom, again with abruptness, he introduces in the verse following today's

Reading: 'It was at this time that Jesus came from Nazareth in Galilee and was baptised by John in the Jordan'.

Nevertheless, brief but vivid, this sketch of John and his ministry is necessary, and serves two purposes.

First, John's appearing illuminates the purpose of the whole Gospel — to answer the question, 'Who is this Jesus of Nazareth?' Secondly, it serves to remind us that (as was the case with John the Baptist) Jesus, and the proclamation of Jesus as the Good News for all the world to hear, is the whole point and purpose and goal of our own appearing in this world.

'A voice cries in the wilderness, "Prepare a way for the Lord".' Here Isaiah is prophesying the return of the Israelites to their homeland out of their exile in Babylon. He proclaims it will be like a new Exodus out of their earlier enslavement in Egypt; and as the Lord himself went before them on that earlier occasion, so he will in the new Exodus which is to come. It is fitting, therefore, that, across the trackless desert, a royal road should be built — a straight path for the Lord.

When Mark makes this 'voice' to be John the Baptist, he makes that 'way' become a moral entity; and John's exhortation to the people urges them to prepare themselves for the coming of the Lord. He urges them to receive Jesus in joy and in faith, for Jesus is *the* Way who, if followed, will lead the whole human race, in the ultimate Exodus — out of a world of the darkness of sin and death into an everlasting homeland of light and life.

The beginning of this final Exodus is the baptism which the 'Someone mightier' than John will confer.

Yet John's baptism was a remarkable creation — far more than a mere ritual purification in that it was unrepeatable, for it symbolised a permanent change of heart. Moreover, it created a real community, a community of 'expecters'. The baptism of the 'Someone mightier', however, creates a community of believers (who are also 'expecters') who have joined Jesus in his Exodus out of this world back to the Father from whom he had come.

To be a Christian is, therefore, to live out the present implications of one's baptism in expectation of its future consumation in glory.

Second Sunday of Advent
Year C
Luke 3:1-6

Luke (in 1:67-79) tells us how, at the naming-ceremony of the new-born John, his father, Zechariah, 'was filled with the Holy Spirit', and spoke this prophecy: 'You, little child, shall be called Prophet of the Most High, for you will go before the Lord to prepare the way for him, to give his people knowledge of salvation through the forgiveness of their sins'. In today's Reading, Luke tells us of the fulfilment of Zechariah's prophecy.

John's appearing and his ministry came to be regarded as the beginning of the Good News. So Peter, when a replacement had to be found for Judas, pointed out that whoever it was had to be 'someone who was with us right from the time when John was baptising'.

Because of the importance of this, Luke gives quite an impressive prologue in which he names representative figures of the whole array of political and religious authority in the Roman and Judean world of those days: and they include those who will encompass the deaths both of John the Baptist and that Jesus whose herald he was and whom he made known when at last he came (cf. Preface).

This prologue also serves to situate Jesus, and the salvation he brings, firmly in the world and in the lives of its people. The coming of Jesus is part of the history of the world, a history which cannot escape being affected by the continuance of faith in him in people of every age.

John was a Voice; Jesus was the Word he proclaimed. The Voice was for a time, and was finally silenced in death; but the Word of the Lord remains for ever — even though heaven and earth (the milieu of human history) should pass away. And all who make their home in his word, by faith in him and by bringing forth fruits worthy of that faith, will share in the eternity of that Word. This is the salvation John proclaims and Jesus grants.

Today, the 'word of the Lord came to John' — the word which brought creation into being, and which commissioned the prophets of old, and does not return without having fulfilled its mission. The word of the Lord is the driving force in the life of John — as it would be in our own lives if only we would have what Isaiah calls 'a disciple's ear to listen'.

To become disciples-who-listen, we have to remove from our hearts and lives those things which (to adapt Isaiah's 'road-makers' imagery) impede a clear sight of God and the salvation he constantly offers — levelling the mountains of our pride, filling up the deep valleys of nurtured resentment and hurt, straightening out our waywardness.

The images do not suggest that doing so in an easy task; nor do they suggest that doing so is an end in itself. We do these things to facilitate the coming of the Word of God to us, and our coming to the Word of God, Jesus.

Second Week
Monday
Luke 5:17-26

Immediately before today's Reading, Jesus heals a leper — a social outcast — and thereby restores him to the human relationships which had been severed by his having contracted the disease. Here, Jesus claims that he has the power to cleanse from sin — thereby restoring sinners to friendship with God, re-establishing the relationship which had been severed by their having sinned.

Jesus' actions as healer make visible his role as reconciler.

The two incidents just mentioned state very directly that the reason for Jesus' advent, his coming into the world, was to effect reconciliation: 'God was in him,' says St Paul, 'reconciling the world to himself'. Reconciliation (peace-making effected through forgiveness) was a fundamental element in Jesus' teaching: 'Offering gifts? First be reconciled to your brother'; and, 'If you will not forgive, your heavenly Father will not forgive you'. Reconciliation was the mission to the world which Jesus gave to his Church: 'We are,' says St Paul, 'ambassadors for Christ . . . and the appeal we make in Christ's name is, Be reconciled to God' (2 Cor 5:19-20).

St Augustine describes the Church as 'constituted on earth as a reconciled world'; and the Church, in turn, must act as 'a reconciling world'. Pope Paul VI, therefore, writes to us all: 'In order to be worthy members of this Body, all must, in fidelity to the baptismal commitment, contribute to preserving it in its original nature as the Community of those who have been reconciled'. He adds that, 'The duty of making peace extends personally to each and every member of the faithful'.

The scene which we contemplate in today's Reading begins serenely enough: Jesus is in a house preaching. Friends of a paralysed man believe that Jesus can cure their friend. Nothing will stop them from coming to Jesus (a determination which should be mine, also). Jesus promptly declares that this man's sins are forgiven.

The reaction of the large number of Pharisees and Doctors of the Law who are among those listening to (but not hearing) Jesus is written all over their faces: easy enough, therefore, to read their thoughts. Jesus challenges them: Yes, it is easy enough to claim to forgive sin, for that is a claim that cannot be verified. But the command to rise and walk is quite another matter. The miracle cannot be denied.

But what it signifies in the spiritual realm can be denied, on the grounds (very limiting to the freedom of God to act graciously) that no man has the power to forgive sin. And so Jesus, who was sent into the world endowed with this power precisely to heal and to reconcile the human race through the forgiveness of sin, is rejected.

Second Week
Tuesday
Matthew 18:12-14

Today we have a Reading which presents us with yet another image or metaphor of the reconciling purpose of Jesus' coming into this world. The Reading is brief, but remembrances of Luke's more detailed version of the parable (in 15:4-7) and of Jesus' extended presentation of himself as the Good Shepherd (in Jn 10:1-16) will assuredly come to mind.

The man who seeks out and brings back the stray is Jesus, who reconciles the stray to the sheepfold (the Community who are one in being reconciled to the Father) and thereby reconciles the stray to the Father. The purpose of every community in which we live — domestic, civil, social, religious — is always, ultimately, reconciliation.

The parable, then, puts into other words what Jesus says of himself (in Lk 19:10): 'I have come to seek and to save that which was lost'. That coming and that purpose were the will of his Father who wishes all whom he has created to be saved, whose will is never 'that one of these little ones should be lost'.

Long ago, Ezekiel (in 34:16) had said: 'It is the Lord who speaks: I shall look for the lost, bring back the stray'. To this end, in that fullness of time which we consider during the final week of Advent, God sends his Son into the world, because 'we like sheep had all gone astray, each taking his own way; and the Lord burdened him (his Servant and Son) with the sins of us all' (Is 53:6).

Seeking, finding, placing on his shoulders and bringing back to the fold the straying sheep also meant for this Good Shepherd of ours the taking upon himself the whole and heavy burden of the sin of the world. But he loves what he carries, and carries what he loves — those lost sheep who are his own in the world; and for their sake he will, with equal love, take upon his shoulder the cross by which they are saved and set free.

'Bear one another's burdens,' says St Paul (in Gal 6:2). To be an imitator of Jesus — who reconciles by bearing others' burdens — is no easy matter; and yet it is the vocation of every member of the Community. (Cf. Pope Paul in yesterday's reflection.) To be an agent of reconciliation can mean, very frequently, real personal suffering; for bearing another's burdens can go far beyond extending sympathy to others. It can mean enduring their sinfulness, as Jesus endures ours.

To do this, we need to follow closely behind Jesus and find strength in the pastures and still waters (Ps 22[23]) to which he leads us — the rich pasturage of his sacramental Body and the refreshing streams of his sacramental Blood.

Second Week
Wednesday
Matthew 11:28-30

In yesterday's Reading, we saw how Jesus is the one who bears our burdens; in today's, he invites us to bear his.

Those burdens of ours which he takes upon himself are crushingly heavy — the weight of a cross and of a world of sin. He takes them from us and lays them upon himself — and, thereby, gives us rest, sets us at ease. 'It was I,' (he says in Ps 81[80]:5) 'who relieved your shoulder of the burden'.

But the burden which he invites us to bear is light. More, it lifts us up, not weighs us down; and the yoke he invites us to bear will (we have his word for it) sit easy on us. ('No rubbing, no galling — guaranteed!': so Jesus in his days as a carpenter might have assured a farmer for whose paired oxen he had made a yoke.)

The image of the Law as a yoke, and the idea of bowing to that yoke in order to find rest (because the Law brings wisdom and wisdom brings peace) were very traditional and well-known ot Jesus' hearers. In fact, however, mainly because of the multiplicity of Pharisaic interpretations of the Law, its observance had become burdensome at the best, and, generally, well-nigh impossible. St Peter acknowledged this when he spoke against the imposition of the Law on gentile Christians — calling it 'a burden neither we nor our ancestors could bear' (cf. Acts 15:10-11). For so many, the rest which the Law promised was not found; and the loving face of the Giver of the Law was obscured. Jesus, however, claims that his yoke is easy, his burden light.

We notice that there *is* a yoke, a burden to be borne. The soul's rest which Jesus promises is not inaction. To be a follower of Jesus means accepting the task he gives us in this life — that is, to live by *his* law. His law, his yoke is the keeping of the two greatest Commandments: to love God with all our heart and mind and strength, and to love our neighbour as ourself.

The reason why his yoke is easy and his burden light is that Jesus himself is our yoke-fellow. By his presence to us, he strengthens us; and he gives us the example of himself — 'meek and humble of heart' — to show us what attitude, what 'the mind which is in us' will enable us to bear that yoke and that burden cheerfully, willingly, lovingly.

It was through the wisdom which it taught that the Law was meant to give rest — peace of heart and soul. Since Jesus is himself the Wisdom of God made flesh, his promise of rest is sure.

Second Week
Thirsday
Thursday
Matthew 11:11-15

Matthew tells us that John the Baptist, when he appeared, wore a garment of camel-hair, and a leather girdle around his waist. The image is meant to call to mind Elijah, for (in 2 Kings 1:8) that great prophet is described as similarly dressed.

The last of the Old Testament prophets, Malachai, concludes his message with the Lord God saying, 'Know that I am going to send you Elijah the prophet before my Day comes'. When, therefore, Jesus here affirms (as he does elsewhere) that John the Baptist, in his role as witness to Jesus, fulfils this prophecy, he is saying that he himself is the embodiment of the Day of the Lord, is himself the embodiment of the Kingdom of God. The Kingdom can be entered only through faith in him; and a person's acceptance or rejection of him *is* God's judgement (the Day of the Lord) on that person.

The 'greater-ness' of John the Baptist, therefore, consists in the superiority of his role over that of the earlier prophets — for he brings to its consummation the whole of ancient prophecy, and announces the inauguration, in Jesus, of the definitive Kingdom of God. So Jesus here affirms; but he adds that the least in the Kingdom (in which everyone is a 'little one' and 'the greatest is the least of all and the servant of all': cf. Mt 18:1-4) is greater than John — for the Kingdom far surpasses the old dispensation which culminates in John. Jesus is not so much contrasting persons as dispensations — the Old Covenant and the New.

Of this Kingdom, Jesus says that it 'suffers violence, and the violent bear it away'. Of the many interpretations of this difficult statement, probably the most personally useful is the view that it refers to the violence one must do oneself in abandoning oneself to Jesus in pure faith — dispensing with all sense-perceptible assurances and securities — and the day to day violence one must do to one's waywardness in trying to live a life in harmony with that faith.

Today's Reading concludes with Jesus' impassioned plea, 'If anyone has ears to hear, let him listen'. It is the plea of the Psalmist long before; 'If today you hear his voice, harden not your hearts' (Ps 95[94]:7-8).

And so we come yet again to pray for that 'disciple's ear' of which Isaiah had spoken (in 50:4). For, as many set eyes on Jesus in his time on earth and yet did not truly see him (and, therefore, rejected him) so, too, many heard the prophets, heard John the Baptist, heard the Word of God made flesh and, not listening, rejected each in turn.

Second Week
Friday
Matthew 11:16-19

We well remember Jesus' words about little children: that the Kingdom of Heaven belongs to such as they; that unless we have a change of heart and become like little children we shall not so much as see the Kingdom; that the greatest in the Kingdom are they who make themselves as little as little children — all which sayings, taken to heart, provide more than sufficient matter for self-reflection.

In today's Reading, however, it is quite another aspect of childhood which Jesus uses to illustrate the point he is making. He points to the petulance of children when they are in a mood not to be pleased by any suggested diversion. And this, too, invites self-questioning: Childlike or childish?

The refusal of the children in the market place (and, surely, in another sense that is where we all are) to 'play at' funerals or weddings symbolises the refusal of Jesus' hearers ('this generation' — and every generation, including our own) to commit themselves either to John the Baptist or to Jesus. John, ascetical himself and summoning people to a change of heart and the 'mourning' which that involves, is simply, but comfortably, dismissed as being possessed by some malign spirit. Jesus comes, with his invitation to a joyful freedom, eating and drinking in fellowship with sinners and welcoming them, and showing an unholy disregard for dietary laws. And he, too, is dismissed, in gross caricature, as 'a glutton and drunkard'.

What is in question is commitment; and, in this context, commitment is no shallow thing. It is a question of whether human judgements such as those pronounced by the contemporaries of John and Jesus are in harmony with the wisdom of God — who sent John and Jesus with the intention that they should be listened to.

'Yet wisdom (the wisdom of God) has been proved right by her actions' — the preaching and the life of John and Jesus, and will be further proved right by the witness of their respective deaths. Luke (in 7:35) prefers to say, 'Yet wisdom has been proved right by *all* her children'; and we are children of wisdom when we heed John's call to repentance, to a profound change of heart, and when we live our lives with Jesus as our model.

The commitment which today's Reading calls for leaves no room for fence-sitting: we are either for or against Christ; we either gather or scatter (cf. Mt 12:30). And this commitment is very like the repentance called for by John: it begins in a moment of profound decision, but is meant to be continually deepened until, in our own dying, we, too, glorify God and vindicate his wisdom.

Second Week
Saturday
Matthew 17:9-13

'As they came down from the mountain': Peter, James and John have just witnessed the Transfiguration of Jesus, and have heard him talking with Moses and Elijah about his own impending death. At the time, they were overwhelmed; but now, everything having returned to normal, they begin to reflect on that experience, and on Jesus' career up to this point — and they find they have a problem.

From that experience they know that Jesus is assuredly the Messiah — the One to whom the Law (in the person of Moses) and all the prophets (in the person of Elijah) bore witness. But if Jesus is the Messiah, why was his coming not heralded by the reappearance of Elijah, as the prophet Malachai had foretold? (cf. Reading: Week 2, Thursday.)

Jesus assures them that the prophecy had been fulfilled in the person of John the Baptist. John had come 'with the spirit and power of Elijah . . . preparing for the Lord a people fit for him'. So the angel of the Lord had announced he would, when declaring to Zechariah that he was to become the father of a son who was to be named John (cf. Lk 1:11-17).

But when John came, 'they did not recognise him'. 'They' are probably the religious leaders of the time, since the people in general did regard John as a prophet. Their leaders, however, did not. We see this, for example, in one of the great confrontation scenes between Jesus and 'the chief priests and elders'. They demand to know by what authority Jesus has expelled

49

the traders from the Temple. Jesus counters with the question: 'John's baptism: did it come from heaven or from man?' They could not say, 'From heaven' — for then their rejection of John would be utterly indefensible. On the other hand, they dared not say, 'From man', for fear of the people, who all held that John was truly a prophet (cf. Mk 11:27-33).

Their failure to 'recognise' (that is, to listen to, to believe in) John, and still more Jesus himself, is akin to Jerusalem's failure to recognise 'the day of its visitation' — a failure over which Jesus shed tears (cf. Lk 19:41).

By this time, John the Baptist was dead, beheaded by King Herod — partly out of the promptings of Herodias, his brother's wife (recalling the persecution of Elijah by Jezebel) and partly out of fear that a popular uprising might take place, proclaiming John as the Messiah, the true King.

Jesus here predicts the same fate for himself — and for the same reason: he, too, will not be 'recognised'. The followers of Jesus can expect the same. Not in a spirit of self-righteousness but in an understanding of the mystery of redemptive suffering, Paul writes to Timothy (in 2 Tim 3:12) that 'anyone who lives in devotion to Christ is certain to be attacked'.

Third Sunday of Advent*
Year A
Matthew 11:2-11

The reason which the Gospels give for John's imprisonment is that he had denounced Herod for divorcing his wife and marrying his sister-in-law, who had likewise divorced her husband. There could have been, also, a strong political reason. People were beginning to conjecture that John might, in fact, be the Messiah, the Christ (although John strenuously denied this) and Herod may have feared a rebellion against his thoroughly unpopular kingship.

Similarly, there are quite different interpretations of John's sending disciples of his to Jesus with the question, 'Are you the One?' Some say that John was beginning to doubt; some say that he was beginning to believe! It could also be that John, who had directed his disciples James and John to Jesus to become his Apostles, was trying to direct the disciples of today's Reading, also, towards a personal encounter with Jesus himself.

Whatever. Today's Reading revolves around belief and disbelief — with, in between, the question of doubt. Jesus is always very gentle with doubt — for the doubter is not yet committed; and a doubter, while in danger of lapsing into disbelief, is equally open to making an act of faith.

When Jesus, therefore, points to the blind seeing and the deaf hearing, he is really talking images of belief ('seeing', 'hearing') and unbelief ('blindness', 'deafness'). His giving sight to the

---

(*) Note: These eight days are called 'Late Advent Weekdays', and the Readings appointed for them take the place of those of the weekdays on which those dates fall. *Sundays are unaffected.* These dates can begin as early as the Third Sunday of Advent and as late as the Saturday after the Third Sunday. This book gives reflections for the weekdays up to that Saturday, as well as for each of the Late Advent Weekdays. The user of this book needs to keep an eye on a liturgical calendar of the current year.

and unbelief ('blindness', 'deafness'). His giving sight to the blind and hearing to the deaf and, above all, his bringing the Good News to the poor, show that he fulfils all the Old Testament expectations of 'the One who was to come'. However, Jesus does not present his fulfilment of these expectations as 'credentials' but simply as an invitation to the one thing necessary — faith.

On the departure of John's disciples, Jesus speaks directly to the crowd regarding the person of John. In doing so, he puts before us three classes of people; and we, perhaps, see something of ourselves in each of them — while hoping to be, in the main, most often included in the third.

The first are the waverers — the 'reeds shaken in the wind'. John was not such; and who would take the trouble ('go out into the wilderness') to listen to such a person? As vacillators, we are ineffectual. The second are they who seek their own comfort and, perhaps, social standing and influence. As self-seekers, we are repellant. Soft clothing and a room in the palace are worlds apart from John in his camel-hair garb out in the wilderness. Thirdly, there are the prophets — those whose speech is in harmony with the breathing of the Spirit, and helps those who seek God to find him.

Yet there is still another class of person, and these Jesus here declares 'blessed'. Those are they who, against all doubt and contentment with soft options, cling to faith in him and his way. It is among these that we pray to be numbered.

Third Sunday of Advent*
Year B
John 1:6-8, 19-28

John's Gospel begins with that great hymn to the eternal Word: 'In the beginning was the Word ... and the Word was

52

God ... and the Word was made flesh and dwelt among us'. The first few verses of today's Reading interrupt the hymn in order to introduce the man who will bear witness to this Word-made-flesh — and to establish at once the incarnate Word's superiority.

The Word is from the beginning, and is God; John is a man, 'sent', in time, by God. Jesus is the light; John is a 'shining lamp' (cf. Jn 5:35); but a lamp has served its purpose once the sun rises. John's task is to bear witness to Jesus: 'He was not the light, only a witness (as we, too, are meant to be) to speak for the light. Light, one would think, is the most seeable of things in itself; but because of man's spiritual blindness it is necessary to draw attention to the presence of the light in order to elicit a response in faith.

Having established, in these three verses, that John is the witness to Jesus, today's Reading then jumps ahead to the manner in which John did bear witness.

The lives of Jesus and John run parallel: both are 'sent' by God; both are subjected to interrogation by unbelieving earthly authorities; and, being rejected, both are done to death by those same earthly powers. (And still in our own day Jesus is on trial in the minds and hearts of people.)

John's testimony is in two parts: who he himself is not, and who Jesus is. Interrogated, he makes three disclaimers. He is not the Christ. He is not Elijah. (It was perhaps his dress which provoked this question, as well as the popular belief that Elijah's reappearance would signal the advent of the Christ.) He is not *the* Prophet foretold by Moses. He is simply a Voice declaring the presence of the Word — a Voice soon to be silenced by the secular power.

In the other Gospels, when asked why he baptises, John promptly asserts the coming of a greater, more cleansing baptism 'with the Spirit and with fire'. Here he contrasts, rather, the insignificance of his baptising in comparison with the crucial importance which the witness he is giving has for his hearers.

But they are deaf (just as we, too, can be selective in when and what we choose to hear in the depths of our hearts, and debate external things).

The Reading concludes with John's declaring that, in regard to Jesus, he, John, is not worthy to perform even the task of a slave. Yet God's call has made him Jesus' witness. So, too, are we — unworthy, yet called.

Third Sunday of Advent*
Year C
Luke 3:10-18

The first half of today's Reading, verses found only in Luke's Gospel, presents us with an aspect of John the Baptist and his preaching which we do not find elsewhere. John's personal asceticism in clothing, diet and lodging was extreme (cf. Mk 1:6) and he taught his disciples the discipline of fasting. (Some people were rather scandalised that Jesus did not teach his disciples the same: cf. Mk 2:18.) But John makes no demands of a physically ascetical kind on those who listen to him, experience a change of heart, and desire to change their lives.

We tend to remember John's preaching chiefly as denunciatory of the 'brood of vipers', and as warning his hearers of 'retribution', 'winnowing' and 'unquenchable fire'. But here we hear him giving people, of a variety of walks of life, advice which is as gentle, and understanding of their lives, as it is sensible, while still demanding — as charity and justice always are demanding since they require the putting aside of selfishness and self-seeking in ourselves.

John's preaching here assumes, as does Vatican II, a 'universal call to holiness'. John and St Francis de Sales (in his *Introduction to the Devout Life*) share the same conviction — that no honest state in life is incompatible with holiness, and that, in fact, the requirements of one's state in life will themselves be sure guides to the way to achieving personal holiness.

John emphasises practical charity — a willingness to give of ourselves and of what we have to others (and to food and clothing we can add time, company, abilities . . .). It is in giving that we strike most deeply at the root of our natural selfishness. He urges contentment with what is sufficient — thereby moderating the desire for, or dependence on the accumulation of material things. He urges the non-abuse, the right use, of whatever authority or power we have (or are in a position to usurp) — meaning that we must, with scrupulous integrity, fulfil our various functions in the various communities to which we belong (domestic, religious, social).

It is a simple yet demanding programme; but also a sure path to genuine holiness of life. It is curious that commentators should refer to the 'shallowness of John's ethical teaching'.

His teaching is, after all, very much what Jesus himself says shall be the crux of the judgement passed on each one of us: 'I was hungry, naked . . . and you did/did not clothe, feed me' (cf. Mt 25:35-46).

More, in its exhortation to contentment and to non-violence it already foreshadows some of what Jesus will say in that Christian Manifesto we call the Beatitudes: 'Blessed are the gentle, the poor in spirit, the peacemaker'.

Third Week
Monday
Matthew 21:23-27

In the chapter of Matthew's Gospel from which today's Reading is taken it is already Holy Week. Jesus has just made his triumphal entry into Jerusalem. He has subsequently purged the Temple of the buyers and sellers who had made his Father's house of prayer into a den of thieves — which is very much like what we do when we allow things to distract us from the real purpose of our own existence. He has allowed the children to hail him as 'Son of David'. And, perhaps worst of all in his interrogators' eyes, he has permitted the blind and the lame to come to him in the Temple (which they were forbidden to enter) where he heals them — signalling that the law was giving way to the graciousness of the Good News.

These are the actions — the 'these things' — regarding which Jesus is questioned as to his authority to perform them. He is asked two things: the nature of his authority, and its source.

When asked such direct questions, Jesus habitually counters with another question. When asked, 'Is it against the law to cure a man on the Sabbath?' Jesus answers, 'If a sheep of yours fell into a hole on the Sabbath, wouldn't you lift it out?' (Cf. Mt 12:9-14.) Asked why did his disciples not wash their hands before eating, Jesus asks in reply why his interrogators nullified the Fourth Commandment when it looked like touching their pockets (cf. Mt 15:1-9).

So here. On none of these occasions is Jesus simply being evasive. He is trying to get his interrogators to look beyond appearances, and, more important, to search their own hearts for the reasons for the judgements they make. This he requires of us, also — not only when it is a matter of observing the actions of others, but even more when it comes to discerning his action in our own lives. Our task is to understand, not to question out of preconceptions.

Jesus' answer, by implication says, that he has, as John the Baptist had, the authority which belongs to an official messenger, and that the source of the authority of both himself and John is God who sent them both. In his refusal to discuss his authority, Jesus is telling his interrogators that, just as they rejected John, so they are rejecting him — and in doing so are rejecting God who sent him.

Jesus is not scoring points. He is appealing to his critics to open their hearts to understand the meaning of John's ministry and his own — that the Kingdom of God has come upon them. He is begging them to look beyond the concrete reality of his actions to discern what those actions say to an open ear, what they clearly manifest to eyes that are not incurably, because deliberately, blind.

Third Week
Tuesday
Matthew 21:28-32

Today's Reading, the 'Parable of the Two Sons', follows immediately upon yesterday's confrontation scene. The parable contains lip-service with actual obedience; but the real point of it is 'repentance' — that radical change of heart which both John and Jesus himself preached. It is only such repentance which enables one who has refused to go into the vineyard (that is to say, has refused the invitation to enter the Kingdom) to change that refusal into compliance.

The Reading begins with, 'What is your opinion?' Timeless, the question can be taken as directly addressing us — the readers of today. At the end, therefore, we are left not with our passing judgement on the two sons but on ourselves. We are left to examine not the behaviour of the two sons but whether or not the way we act matches what we say we believe.

The first son is variously described as 'impudent' or 'rebellious'. He invites the designation 'impudent' since he gives his father, who has addressed him tenderly as 'son', no correspondingly affectionate title in return. He deserves the designation 'rebellious' because of his flat refusal to do what his father asks of him — until he has a change of heart and accedes to his father's request.

The second son, addressed in precisely the same words as the first, is docile to the point of exaggeration, calling his father

'Sir' — a docility certainly not shown in deed. He is one of those of whom Jesus says, 'It is not those who say to me, "Lord, Lord" who will enter the Kingdom of Heaven, but the person who does the will of my Father in heaven' (Mt 7:21). He is like the anonymous 'you' whom James (in 2:14-20) addresses: 'I will prove to you that I have faith by showing you my good deeds. Now you, without any good deeds to show, prove to me that you have faith'. He is reproached by God with, 'This people honours me with only lip-service, while its heart is far from me' (Is 29:13).

Jesus' interrogators have to acknowledge that the first son was the one who *did* his father's will; but they choose to ignore the fact that it was a change of heart which made this so. Jesus makes three appeals to them.

First, he reminds them that they had the witness of John. John was 'a pattern of true righteousness' — that is to say, was a holy man himself and one who showed the true path to righteousness to whoever would listen to him. Then Jesus asks them to consider the phenomenon, that marvel of grace, that the — in their estimation — lowest of the low, the tax collectors and prostitutes, did listen to John's call, and acted on it.

The third appeal is not put into words. It is simply Jesus himself, standing before them — as he stands before me now.

Third Week
Wednesday
Luke 7:19-23

Today's Reading is Luke's version of the first half of the passage from Matthew set down for the Third Sunday of Advent, Year A.

Picturing the scene as Luke presents it, we see the arrival of John's disciples, and hear them put John's question to Jesus. From Jesus we hear no reply. He simply turns to cure 'many people of diseases and afflictions and of evil spirits, and give the gift of sight to many who are blind'. It is only after having done these things that he speaks; and his speaking is a drawing of the messengers' attention to the fact that these works of his indicate that he is fulfilling the expectations of the Old Testament regarding the One who was to come.

Jesus is reminding them of, especially, Isaiah: 'He has sent me to bring good news to the poor, to bind up hearts that are broken . . . to comfort all those who mourn' (cf. 61:1-3); 'Your dead will come to life' (26:19); 'The eyes of the blind shall be opened, the ears of the deaf unsealed; then the lame shall leap like a deer, and the tongues of the dumb shall sing for joy' (35:5-6).

This was what the messengers were to report back to John.

In the reflection for the Third Sunday, Year A, three commonly held explanations of John's sending this embassy were given: that John was beginning to doubt; that he was beginning to believe; that he wanted his disciples to have a personal encounter with Jesus.

There is a fourth opinion: that John was simply puzzled at what the disciples reported to him in prison regarding Jesus' works and words. His words were gentle, his actions merciful; and at the same time he welcomed sinners and ate with them.

All this was so puzzlingly different from what John had assumed when he was preaching about 'the retribution that is coming': '. . . he will baptise with the Holy Spirit and fire. His winnowing-fan is in his hand; he will clear his threshing-floor and gather his wheat into the barn; but the chaff he will burn in a fire that will never go out' (cf. Mt 3:1-12).

Jesus message to John, 'Blessed is the man who does not lose faith in me', says, virtually, 'Yes, I am he — even if I am not as you expected'.

The whole incident warns us against holding preconceptions as to how Jesus will (or, as we think, should) act in our lives — especially if we are feeling 'imprisoned'. For if we do, we shall miss the many advents of Jesus into our life and, like Jerusalem (cf. Lk 19:44) will fail to recognise the day of our being visited.

Third Week
Thursday
Luke 7:24-30

Taking up where yesterday's left off, today's Reading gives us Luke's version of the second half of that same passage from Matthew set down for the Third Sunday of Advent, Year A.

Today, Jesus questions people concerning their understanding of John the Baptist and his mission. In doing so, he says, 'This is he of whom it is written, ''Behold, I am sending my messenger before you, and he will prepare a way for you'' '. 'It is written,' Jesus says — quoting the last of the Old Testament prophets, Malachai (in 3:1). But if we turn to Malachai, we find that what the prophet actually said was, 'Behold, I am sending my messenger before *me*, and he will prepare *my* way before *me*'.

Malachai is speaking of the coming of the Christ — the ultimate messenger of God to mankind, God's own Word made flesh, and both the bearer of and the essence of God's Good News to mankind. Jesus, when he quotes this prophecy to show the significance of John, changes it and makes John the messenger — the herald, therefore, of Jesus himself as the incarnation of 'God's visiting his people'.

Jesus proclaims an identification between John and himself, for John had a mission from God just as Jesus himself has. John has a share, not usurped but God-given, in the mission which Jesus himself has from God. This identification which he proclaimed existed between himself and John by reason of their both being sent by God, Jesus raises, among his followers, to a pitch of undreamed of intimacy.

By Baptism we are so made members of Christ, so personally identified with Jesus, that when Saul persecutes his followers Jesus reproaches him for persecuting Jesus himself (cf. Acts 9:4); and to neglect works of mercy towards our fellow human beings is to disregard Jesus himself (cf. Mt 26:31-46).

Members of Christ, we share in the priesthood of Christ and in his appointed mission to the human race. Anointed with the Holy Spirit, as Jesus was in preparation for his public ministry, we are, in our daily lives, witnesses to the fact that 'God has visited his people', just as Jesus is witness to, and is the incarnation of that visitation.

Since we are members of Christ and one with Christ, we live by the life of Christ himself. It is this life in us — because it is both invincible and self-sacrificial — which saves us from being either of the two things most inimical to our witnessing to Jesus — to be waverers ('reeds shaken by the wind') or self-indulgent self-seekers ('those who go in for fine clothes and live luxuriously, and are found in palaces').

Third Week
Friday
John 5:33-36

Since tomorrow must necessarily begin or fall within the series of 'Late Advent Weekdays', December 17th to 24th, there is no Liturgy of the Word for the Saturday of the Third Week. Consequently, today's Reading (if used at all) brings to a conclusion the two weeks of Advent devoted to the witness given by John the Baptist.

That conclusion is absolute in its finality, for it is Jesus' own analysis of the significance of John's witness. So, too, is Jesus' judgement on the witness we ourselves give both absolute and final.

In the few verses comprising today's Reading, Jesus makes three points regarding John's testimony. First, 'he gave testimony to the truth'. John called Jesus 'Son of God', 'Lamb of God', and the one who would 'baptise with the Holy Spirit'. These titles, therefore, truly indicate aspects of who Jesus is.

61

Secondly, Jesus asserts that he does not depend on John's or any other human testimony. Who Jesus is validates John's testimony, not vice-versa. Finally, Jesus says that he reminds his hearers of John's witness not for his own vindication but for their 'salvation'.

He reminds them that just as Elijah is described in Ecclesiasticus 48:1 so John was 'a lighted lamp'. (But he was not the light: cf. Third Sunday, Year B.) Those who heard John 'rejoiced in the light he gave' — but only 'for a time'. The novelty soon wore off for those 'itching ears' (cf. 2 Tim 4:3). They, for a while, enjoyed hearing John's preaching, but totally ignored what John was testifying to. Jesus reminds them of their past enthusiasm in the hope that, finally, they might attend to the object of John's witness, and so come to 'salvation' through faith in Jesus.

There is a warning for all of us in this. Even the most religious of enthusiasms runs a two-fold danger: it may be short-lived, and die before producing those fruits which guarantee the genuiness of faith; or it may, in fact, be a real stumbling block if we simply revel in the experience of enthusiasm and fail to consider the essential reality of what we are being enthusiastic about. Yet again we hear echoes of, 'Lord, Lord'.

Jesus then declares that there is a testimony to him greater than John's, and that is the works that his Father has given him to carry out. Since these works are the will of his Father, and the gift of his Father, they are evidence of his unique relationship with his Father — a relationship to which the Father himself testifies in so empowering Jesus. His works are more than simply miracles, more than signs, more than evidence that Jesus fulfills all the Old Testament expectations regarding the One who was to come. They are evidence of the Father's acting in a unique way through his unique Son. As Jesus says at the beginning of this long passage (in verse 19): 'the Son can do nothing by himself; he can do only what he sees the Father doing: and whatever the Father does the Son does too'.

PHASE THREE
Fourth Week of Advent

An Over-view
The Coming of the Saviour

The last eight days of Advent are a time of preparation for and expectation of the birth of Jesus on Christmas Day; and on those days, therefore, our Readings come from those events in the infancy narratives of Matthew and Luke which lead up to that birth. Thus (including the Readings for the Fourth Sunday) we have: Matthew's genealogy of the human descent of our Saviour; the annunciations to Zechariah, to Mary, and to Jospeh; the visitation of Elizabeth by Mary, and Mary's canticle, the *Magnificat*; the birth of John the Baptist, and Zechariah's canticle, the *Benedictus* — the last gospel Reading we hear before the narrative of the birth of Jesus. Very suitably, we join in saying, 'Blessed be the Lord God', even now, for what is to happen tomorrow in token of what will happen at the end of the ages, the Coming of Christ — tomorrow, to share with us our broken humanity; at the end, to bestow on us the immortality and the glory that are his.

As, day by day, these great moments in God's plan of salvation unfold before us, we pray to be drawn to rejoice in his merciful love and in his power to save. These great moments are also intensely human happenings; and so we pray, also, to experience something of what the persons concerned experienced, and to see how their experiences and their responses are relevant to our own day to day lives.

In some places, there used to be celebrated at this time of the year a feast called 'The Expectation of the Blessed Virgin

Mary'. The object of the feast was to contemplate Mary as 'she pondered in her heart' the events of the past nine months, and looked forward 'in joyful hope to the coming of our Saviour, Jesus Christ'. This contemplation of Mary under these aspects is the best preparation of our hearts to receive the Christmas mystery which we ourselves can make; for Mary is, supremely, the Woman of Advent, the Lady-in-waiting.

The season of Advent is all about waiting. The world waited for its Saviour to come; the world waits for him to come again. And all of us who have faith in both that first coming and the second, also wait for him to come to us in the here and now of the daily events of our lives, to come with his healing, his strength, his light, and his personal, intimate love for each one of us.

For this his constant coming, we must be prepared — so that we are not, like Jerusalem, 'unaware of the day of its being visited' (Lk 19:42); and for his constant coming we must also long, otherwise we are undeserving of it. So à Kempis writes in his *Imitation of Christ* (3, 21, 4): 'Come, oh come . . . for you are my joy, and without you my table is empty'.

The chief obstacles to our sustaining this very necessary heart's desire are discouragement and doubt: discouragement which springs from the apparent deferment of his coming; doubt that he comes at all. Patience is the remedy for discouragement; faith the only remedy for doubt.

Of both patience and faith, Mary in this time of her Expectation, Mary, the Lady-in-waiting, is our model. From the moment of our first coming to faith in him, Christ is within us; but it takes time before he is fully formed within us, and we ourselves grow to our full stature in Christ (cf. Eph 4:13). But just so was the case with Mary, the Advent Woman.

Fourth Sunday of Advent
Year A
Matthew 1:18-24

Whatever school of thought one may lean towards regarding the reason for Joseph's quandary, the fact is that he is in a quandary. How much he knows, the various possibilities he may conjecture — these things we simply do not know. His problem is that he must act — but act in character; and his is the character of 'a just man', an upright, religious man — a man, that is to say, accustomed to listening for, hearing, and then acting on what he believes to be God's word to him.

Joseph has a problem. He does the first thing discernment of it suggests: he 'sleeps' on it. That is to say, he does nothing in haste. And it is while he is sleeping that his human considerations are broken in upon by a divine intervention, a dream — so often in the religious tradition of his people a means of God's communicating with the children of his making.

Joseph is a perfect example of true discipleship. He has 'a disciple's ear to listen', and his obedience is prompt and exact; and, having listened and obeyed, he gives himself to a life-long service to Jesus, neither asking nor knowing just what that will entail. Joseph's promptness to obey reveals that he is one in heart with Mary in her, 'I am the handmaid of the Lord; let it be done ...'. He has in himself already 'the mind that was in Christ Jesus', expressed in both his prayer and his agony — 'Your will be done'.

While in this passage Matthew acknowledges Joseph's probity and the gentleness of his heart, he is concerned, rather, with Joseph's place in God's salvific plan. (And we, too, have a place in it.) By not repudiating his wife, and by giving the child the name which God had already given him, Joseph ensures Jesus' rightful place in the line of David.

The name, Jesus, is the name which is above all names, the name to which everything in heaven and on earth pays homage (cf. Phil 2:9). In keeping with its meaning, 'Yahweh saves', it is the only name given to mankind through which they can be saved (cf. Acts 4:12). But despite its majesty, it is also a very homely name, and very dear.

This Jesus is also our Emmanuel — 'God with us'; and he is 'with us' precisely in order to 'save'.

Matthew concludes his gospel with the words, 'Know that I am with you always; yes, to the end of time'. Mark ends his gospel with a picture of the Apostles going forth to preach, 'the Lord working with them'.

God's presence to us is not static; it is dynamic, creative — or would be if we placed no obstacles in its way.

Fourth Sunday of Advent
Year B
Luke 1:26-38

Contemplating this scene and listening to the dialogue between Mary and Gabriel, we learn what is going on behind the scenes, so to speak. God, in his infinite mercy, is bringing about the salvation of the human race; and, in his infinite wisdom, is making human cooperation an essential part of his saving activity. And as we ourselves are the recipients of that mercy, so must we be also actively cooperative with that salvific will.

Here, Mary is 'the attentive Virgin'. With faith she receives the Word of God, and conceives the Word of God — having with love submitted herself wholly to God's will, putting herself completely and unreservedly at his disposal.

Here, Mary is not only 'the handmaid of the Lord'; she is also the Bridal Chamber of the Lord in which the Word is wedded to flesh in so wonderful a way that, in that union, humankind becomes a new creation. The Word was made flesh so that all flesh could be united to the Word. He took to himself the human nature that belongs to us in order to bestow on us a share in what belongs to him — divine life.

Here, Mary becomes the chalice of the blood of our redemption, the mould of the manhood of Christ, the fruitful field in which was planted the mystic Vine, whose branches we are (cf. Jn 15:5).

Thus becoming the Mother of Christ, Mary becomes the Mother of the Church which is the Body of Christ, and thereby becomes the Mother of all of us who are members of that Body — all of us whom Christ identifies with himself, and with whom he shares his own life.

Mary, the Mother of Christ, becomes, therefore, a model for both the Church, the Body of Christ, and for each one of us who are members of Christ. So Vatican II says, 'It is by contemplating and imitating Mary that the Church herself becomes a mother, and by accepting God's word in faith, as Mary did, keeps whole and pure the fidelity which she, the Church, has pledged to Christ, her Bridegroom'. Thus, in the language of the early Fathers, the Church, too, becomes the Mother of Christ, for 'The Church never ceases to give birth to the Word, and brings forth Christ when she teaches the nations'. And, 'It would be wrong to proclaim the incarnation of the Son of God from the holy Virgin without admitting also his incarnation in the Church'.

Like Mary, each of us is greeted by God, and called upon first to conceive Christ in our hearts by faith and by obedience to the Word, to nurture with love the Christ-life within us, and then bring him forth into the world around us, to make him visible to the world through the Christlikeness of our way of life in what we say and in what we do.

Fourth Sunday of Advent
Year C
Luke 1:39-45

Mary, having conceived the Word, responds promptly to Gabriel's revelation to her that her aged and childless kinswoman, Elizabeth, is now in the sixth month of pregnancy, and sets out as quickly as she can for the hill country of Judah. (Truly, 'Beautiful upon the mountains are the feet of one who brings good news, heralds peace, brings happiness, proclaims salvation' [Is 52:7].)

In the Visitation, Jesus the Sanctifier (cf. Heb 2:11) fulfils Gabriel's prophecy (in Lk 1:15) that the Precursor would be 'filled with the Holy Spirit even from his mother's womb'; and the first to whom John announces the advent of Jesus is his own mother. Mary speaks a greeting; John leaps in the womb; and Elizabeth is filled with the Holy Spirit.

Since, 'without faith it is impossible to please God' (cf. Heb 11:6), faith is the foundation of our lives: faith in the sense of unshakeable belief in God and in the truth he reveals through his word; faith in the sense of absolute trust that God will fulfil his promises; faith in the sense of complete acceptance of all that God permits befall us.

Of faith such as this, Mary is the First Lady; she is the Woman of Faith, the true Daughter of Abraham, our father in faith. Among the first to whom the greatness of Mary is revealed was Elizabeth. It was not of herself but 'being filled with the Holy Spirit' that Elizabeth cried out, 'How have I deserved that the mother of my Lord should visit me? And blessed is she who believed that the word the Lord spoke to her would be fulfilled'.

The Old Testament title, 'Mother of my Lord', meant the Queen Mother. Elizabeth, therefore, is struck by the honour done her in Mary's visiting her. But when she wishes to name the personal greatness of Mary her rare spiritual insight takes her beyond the physical fact of motherhood to the depths of Mary's soul: 'And blessed is she who believed . . .'

From the start, the Gospel presents Mary as the Woman of Faith. And it is his mother's faith that Jesus himself praises when, a woman having cried out, 'Blessed is the womb that bore you', he responds with, 'Blessed, rather, are they who hear the word of God and keep it' (cf. Lk 11:28). Again, Jesus says, 'Whoever does the will of my Father in heaven is my mother' (cf. Mk 3:35).

It was through her faith in God's word and her readiness to do God's will that Mary conceived Christ in herself, and brought him to others. It is only through a like faith and obedience that we can conceive Christ in ourselves and be in a position to bring him to others. Thus Mary stands before us as the model disciple, and in herself she shows what is the essence of discipleship — faith and obedience.

December 17th
Matthew 1:1-17

Recently (3rd Sunday: Year A; 3rd Week: Wednesday) we have twice read Jesus' word of encouragement to John the Baptist in his imprisonment: 'Blessed is the one who does not lose faith in me'. The opening line of Matthew's gospel tells us the reason why.

To lose faith in Jesus is to fail to see that God is faithful to his promises, and has, in Jesus, brought them to fulfilment. Jesus is the goal towards which tends all the saving activity of God which the Old Testament records and celebrates.

'A genealogy of Jesus Christ, son of David, son of Abraham.'

Matthew is saying that Jesus is the fulfilment of God's covenant with Abraham — 'to bless the nations through his descendants' (cf. Gen 22:18), and of his covenant with David — 'Your House and your sovereignty will always stand secure before me, and your throne be established for ever' (2 Sam 7:11). Hence Jesus says, 'Abraham rejoiced to think he would see my day' (Jn 8:56); and in Luke's account of the annunciation to Mary (in 1:32-33), Gabriel proclaims, 'The Lord God will give him the throne of his ancestor, David'.

In this genealogy, Matthew is concerned with the earthly origins of Jesus, and with Jesus' legal right to be designated 'of the House of David'. In his narrative of the annunciation to Joseph (4th Sunday: Year A) Matthew is concerned with Jesus' divine origin — although even here there is a foreshadowing of this (in 15-16) where it is said that Joseph was the husband of Mary, but not the father of Jesus. On these two pillars rests that most fundamental affirmation of our faith: 'Jesus Christ, true God and true man'.

Hence Thomas can touch the wounds in the humanity of Jesus and acknowledge the glory of his Godhead. The dust of our earth once covered the feet of him who made the earth. He who fed thousands himself experienced hunger, and is himself the Bread of Life come down from heaven. Thirsty, he asked the Samaritan woman for water to drink, offering in return the waters of salvation. He knew what it was to be homeless, but invites us to make our home in his words of eternal life. He wept at the grave of his friend Lazarus, but showed that he himself is the Resurrection and the Life.

'Whom the Virgin bore, the Virgin adored', saying (as we, too, can say), 'This is flesh of my flesh, and bone of my bones' (cf. Gen 2:23), but also, 'My Lord and my God' (cf. Jn 20:28). This is why we look forward to the coming of Jesus on Christmas Day, for then we shall see God indisolubly wedded to our own and self-same human nature; and that union, and the pledge it gives us of future glory is why we look forward to the Day of the Lord's second Coming.

December 18th
Matthew 1:18-24

This Reading, if used, is also the Reading for the Fourth Sunday of Advent: Year A, for which a Reflection has already been given.

December 19th
Luke 1:5-25

It is very difficult to read the narrative of the annunciation to Zechariah without constantly thinking of the annunciation to Mary (4th Sunday: Year B); and Luke probably intends this, just as he clearly intends us to recall the very similar annunciations in the Old Testament: to Sarah and Abraham — aged and childless but destined to become the father of all believers (cf. Gen 17:1-8), to the childless wife of Manoah who subsequently becomes the mother of Samson, the people's deliverer (Jud 13:1-7), and to Hannah, the mother-to-become of the prophet Samuel (1 Sam 1:9-18) — she whose canticle (1 Sam 2:1-10) so reminds us of Mary's (cf. December 22nd).

The two annunciations which Luke relates are not only in line with the great salvific interventions of God in the past, they bring that intervention to its goal in the God-man, Jesus. They also serve to emphasise the different origins of John and Jesus, and their different (if associated) missions — John's to prepare the people, through repentance, to receive salvation, Jesus' to bring salvation.

Perhaps what most readily springs to mind in this movement from one annunciation to the other is that the so similar annunciations have so different an outcome for their recipients,

Mary and Zechariah. Zechariah questions how, in this regard, the word of the Lord shall be fulfilled — and is struck dumb. Mary asks the same question and receives the answer — 'The Holy Spirit will come upon you . . . ' Wherein lies the difference between words so alike that they should have so different an outcome?

Zechariah's question voices disbelief, and seeks explanation; Mary's question proclaims immediate belief, and seeks only illumination. Disbelief cannot be dispelled by explanation; but the darkness of faith can be illuminated by the light of the Holy Spirit, who guides our minds into all truth (cf. Jn 16:13) not by explanation but by illumination, not by information but by wisdom.

Since Jesus himself does so — 'My God, my God, why have you forsaken me?' (Mt 27:46) — we, too, may make the prayer of questioning. But if it is an expression of disbelief we cannot expect to have our lips opened in prayer (You will be dumb), or ourselves enlightened. But if our questioning is, in fact, an act of faith, it is also a prayer — in response to which the Spirit will come.

And we know that our questioning is in faith when the heart is open to receive, by way of an answer, even a further call to deeper and darker faith, and to a more complete abandonment of ourselves to our Father's will.

December 20th
Luke 1:26-38

This Reading, if used, is also the Reading for the Fourth Sunday of Advent: Year B, for which a Reflection has already been given.

December 21st
Luke 1:39-45

*This Reading, if used, is also the Reading for the Fourth
Sunday of Advent: Year C, for which a Reflection has already
been given.*

December 22nd
Luke 1:46-56

As we reflect on Mary's canticle, we might do well to see
her standing before us and inviting us to join with her, saying,
'Proclaim with me the greatness of the Lord; together, let us
extol his name' (Ps 34[33]:3). For we do not reflect on Mary's
Magnificat simply to admire it, but for it to help us (capturing
something of its exultancy) to make our own joyful noise to
the Lord (cf. Ps 66[65]:1) as we, also, reflect on the 'great things'
God has done for us. In gratitude for all that the Lord has done
for us, we should be forever exhorting ourselves, 'Bless the Lord,
my soul. All my being, bless his name. Bless the Lord, my soul,
and remember all his kindness' (Ps 103[102]:1-2).

Mary breaks into song in response to Elizabeth's words, 'How
have I deserved that the Mother of my Lord should visit me?
And blessed is she who believed'. If Elizabeth sees herself
blessed in Mary's visiting her, how much the more Mary knows
herself blessed in the Lord himself visiting her. If Elizabeth
praises Mary's faith, how much the more Mary knows to praise
God's grace which enabled her to respond to him with such
faith, and with such salvific effect.

Mary begins with the particular — herself, and her own personal experience of the graciousness of the mercy of God which

impelled him to look with favour on her lowliness — not for any merits of her own but because 'God resists the proud, but favours the humble' (Jas 4:6). This is a universal proposition, as Mary next proclaims: 'And his mercy is from age to age for those who fear him'.

When Mary says that the Lord *has* shown, routed, pulled down, exalted, filled, and so on, she is using the language of prophecy which, looking forward to the End, speaks of things, then to be made manifest, as if they had already happened — as, indeed, in God's merciful design, they have begun. Mary is saying that what she, personally, has experienced of God's dealings with her is true, also, of all his dealings with all who reverence him.

Mary is not making a statement about political, social or economic revolution — let alone advocating such. 'He', the Lord, is the active 'doer' of all the 'doing' statements she makes. Mary is simply making a supremely confident act of faith that God's values, so different from those of an unregenerate world, will prevail.

Luke is probably telling his readers/hearers that this is the way things should already be in a genuinely Christian community — where all who are experiencing any kind of poverty, powerlessness, hunger or need are cherished and relieved; and where any kind of 'authority' is essentially simply a greater opportunity to serve.

At this point, we examine our conscience in regard to the various 'communities' in which we live and act.

December 23rd
Luke 1:57-66

Yesterday's Reading concluded with saying that Mary remained with Elizabeth about three months. The phrase reminds us of 2 Sam 6:11 where it is said that the Ark of the Covenant was in the house of Obed-Edom for three months, and the Lord blessed Obed-Edom and his whole family. What blessings, then, for Zechariah and Elizabeth to have under their roof the true Ark of the Covenant, Mary.

The Ark of old was made of incorruptible wood, overlaid with purest gold. It carried within itself the Tables of the Law and a jar of the Manna which fed our fathers in the desert; while upon it, between the overshadowing wings of sculptured cherubim, was the Mercy Seat, of which God said, 'There shall I come to meet you'.

Mary became the Ark of the New Covenant when the Holy Spirit came upon her and the power of the Most High over-shadowed her. In her, God most assuredly came to meet his people when, in her, the Word was made flesh. And she, ever-virgin and never to know the corruption of the grave, and more than golden with the glory of fullness of grace, carried within herself the Bread of Life come down from heaven, the Blood of the new and everlasting Covenant, and the Giver of the law of love.

Undoubtedly, Mary would have stayed for the birth of Elizabeth's child, John, and the naming of him eight days later. It is the naming rather than the birth which engages Luke's attention; for the circumstances of controversy and wonderment which surround that naming foreshadow the controversy and wonderment which will be engendered when the one named begins to fulfil his role as Precursor of the Lord.

Elizabeth says, 'He is to be called John'. Such a departure from tradition cannot go unchallenged, and so Zechariah is appealed to. He writes, 'His name *is* John' — for (as was the case with Jesus) the name had already been given him before ever he was conceived and came to be. In neither case are the parents given any say in the naming of their respective sons; for just as the giving of those sons is not in the natural order of things but the result of divine intervention, so, too, the naming of them and the assigning them their mission in life are purely God's doing.

It is God who is the source of our life, also; and it is only by his grace that we have the name of 'Christian'. And the mission he gives each of us in life is, in the words of a Collect, 'to strive to be worthy of our name of "Christian" and to reject everything opposed to it'.

December 24th
Luke 1:67-79

In tomorrow's Reading it will be given to the angels of God to sing the birth of God's own Son, and to announce his mission as Saviour. Today, it is the father of the child, his tongue now loosed, who sings the appropriate canticle. The canticle falls into two sections: a hymn of praise of God, and an address to the little child himself.

Zechariah blesses God for this clear evidence that God has visited his people — in accordance with the words of his ancient prophets, in fulfilment of his promises, in fidelity to his covenants. From the present, Zechariah looks back to the past to David, and further back to Abraham — declaring that God's merciful purpose has always been at work, as it still is.

And what is true of God's people is true of each of us. From the beginning of our life, God has been leading us by the hand to the eternal salvation his mercy has destined for us, even in the times of our reluctance, even rebellion — in which, too, we see ourselves in God's Old Testament people. Much better for us were we sincerely to resolve 'to serve him in holiness and virtue, living in his presence all the days of our life', aware of his faithfulness, remembering his manifold mercies, and singing his praises.

In addressing his child, Zechariah moves from praise to prophecy. No doubting now the words addressed to him by Gabriel at the annunciation of John's conception! In fact, Zechariah describes the future mission of John in much the same way as Gabriel did when the angel said, 'He will turn many of the sons of Israel to the Lord their God, and he will go before him ... to turn ... the disobedient to the wisdom of the just, to make ready for the Lord a people prepared'.

All that John is to achieve, Zechariah says, stems from the 'tender mercy of God' through his bringing 'from on high, the Rising Sun, to visit us and give light' — Jesus, the Light of the world.

Just as the sun is, for all the world, the sum and source of its warmth and light, so is Jesus, the Sun of Justice, the sum and source of justice, of righteousness for all human kind. The Word made flesh is 'full of grace and truth'; 'and of his fullness we have all received' (cf. Jn 1:14, 16) — so that 'we who were once darkness have become light in the Lord', as St Paul says (cf. Eph 5:8), adding, 'Be like children of light, for the effects of the light are seen in complete goodness, and right living, and truth'.